Table of Contents

Introduction 4
Tips for Success 8

Breakfast 10

Ham and Cheese Waffles 11 • Cornmeal Waffles 12 • Chicken and Chile Quiche Lorraine 13 • Canadian Bacon and Potato Bake 14 • Ham and Cheese Free-Form Tart 15

Appetizers 16

Cheese and Spinach-Stuffed Free-Form Tart 17 • Sausage Balls 18 • Mini Cheese Quiches 19 • Squash Squares 20 • Chinese Dumplings 21

Sandwiches 22

Sausage in a Sarape 23 • Pizza Pronto 24 • Salmon with Dill and Cream Cheese Focaccia 25 • Hot Barbecue Biscuits 26 • Tuna Melts 27 • Cheese-Filled Swirls 28 • Cheese and Spinach-Stuffed Loaf 29 • Four Seasons Pizza 30

Entrées 32

Spinach, Ham, and Cheese Braid 33 • Cornmeal-Topped Beef with Sausage and Cheese Casserole 34 • Salmon and Mushroom Deep-Dish Pie 36 • Oven-Fried Chicken Fingers 38 •

Hot Chicke[...] [...] Chicken and Broccoli Casserole with Biscuits 40 • Chili Cobbler 42 • Spinach and Cheese Pie 44 • Chicken and Vegetable Deep-Dish Pie 46 • Beef and Vegetable Dumpling Stew 47 • Turkey and Ham Pie with Biscuits 48 • Sunday Chicken Casserole with Puff Pastry Crust 49 • Overnight Free-Form Onion and Mozzarella Pies 50 • Meatball Pizza Casserole 51 • Red and White Clam Pizza 52 • Top Hat Sloppy Joes 53 • Shrimp Cakes with Hollandaise Sauce en Croûte 54

Cakes and Breads 56

Orange-Butter Sweet Cake 57 • Cinnamon-Raisin Honey Cake 58 • Streusel-Topped Cake 59 • Fried Apple-Topped Cake 60 • Cold-Oven Breakfast Cake 61 • Dried Cherry Scones 62 • Pecan Sticky Buns 63 • Spicy Puff Pastry Cheese Twists 64 • Three-Ingredient Beer Bread 65 • Poppy Seed-Onion Loaf 66 • Mexican Cheese Bread 67

Bar Cookies and Desserts 68

Chocolate Chip Caramel-Filled Bars 69 • Oatmeal Raisin Chocolate-Filled Bars 70 • Pecan Pie Bars 71 • Rustic Free-Form Fruit Pies 72 • Lemon Cheesecake Tassies 73

Notes 74
Acknowledgements 80

Introduction

A simple act of forgetfulness thousands of years ago changed bread making (and, for that matter, beer brewing) forever. The theory is that someone back in ancient Egypt accidentally left flour and water sitting unattended in the hot sun. Upon returning, he found the ingredients had expanded and a strange alcoholic smell was wafting from the mass. Up to that point, yeast was unknown to these early cooks, but after that discovery it became an integral ingredient.

Yeast gave airiness and lightness to dense flatbread—a mainstay for Egyptians and Romans alike. It also opened up a world of ideas for developing distinctive loaves. Yeast-raised breads offered a culinary venue for people to express their traditions and heritage, associating particular breads with distinct geographic regions. There were Italian pizza flatbreads, yard-long narrow French baguettes, potato and herb-filled Georgian breads, Asian naan, Ethiopian spice breads, Armenian lavash, and Mediterranean pitas, to name just a few. For hundreds of generations, yeast was the only form of leavening known, but that didn't prevent early cooks from experimenting with a multitude of other ingredients in an effort to create appetizing dishes and appealing breads.

In other parts of the world, observant, creative peoples—such as those from the British Isles, Persia (today's Iran), Georgia, Italy, Finland, and Norway—used pearl ash, derived from wood ashes, to produce their special versions of breads. Pearl ash created bubbles of carbon dioxide when mixed with a wet acidic ingredient, such as vinegar, buttermilk, yogurt, or sour milk. Its discovery brought about numerous quick breads, enjoyed for their unusual tangy flavor and for the little time required to mix the ingredients and shape and bake the dough. This early form of baking soda created a vast category embracing Irish soda bread; Finnish barley bread; Italian piadina; Scottish bannock, oatmeal farls, and scones; as well as Native American fry breads. Centuries later, other American quick breads, such as southern biscuits and cornbread, could be prepared and on the table in the blink of an eye.

Both of these leavening agents had drawbacks because they left the home baker with uncertainties and failures.

Yeast was finicky, requiring extra care and coddling. If the dissolving water was too hot, the yeast died; if it was cold, it took forever to act. Furthermore, yeast breads required kneading, a laborious process designed to make a fine, evenly textured bread with carbon dioxide-filled air pockets. Baking soda wasn't much easier because using too much resulted in coarsely grained, yellowish baked goods with a bitter flavor. Home baking remained a doubtful proposition at best, but help was on the way.

Referred to as "portable yeast," baking powder was created in 1855 by combining baking soda with cream of tartar, a natural fruit acid principally obtained from the juice of grapes. Baking powder guaranteed bakers the assurance that when their cakes, quick breads, and other doughy foods came in contact with oven heat, they would "bake up light and right." Home bakers sang the praises of the new product. At last, they were free from worry, flops, and guessing, and one wondered if baking could get any better.

In 1930, when the dark clouds of the Great Depression gripped America, Mabel White Holmes devised a baking mix formula that only needed liquid added to make fluffy biscuits. She called her revolutionary product Jiffy Baking Mix because it made biscuits just that fast. Jiffy Baking Mix contains the same ingredients today as it did in the beginning: flour, shortening, sugar, phosphate, dry defatted milk, salt, and soda. The product was so well received that it inspired Holmes to create other convenience baking products.

Holmes and her husband owned the Chelsea Flourmill in Chelsea, Michigan, giving them the resources and an ideal environment to proof her array of ideas. Shortly after the initial biscuit mix success, Holmes introduced pie crust mix, corn muffin mix, and an assortment of cake mixes to a nation that happily gobbled them up.

The following year, 1931, General Mills began marketing Bisquick baking mix, inspired by an experience Carl Smith, a General Mills executive, had when he ordered biscuits with his meal in a Pullman train dining car. Bowled over by how swiftly the fresh, hot biscuits arrived, Smith found out the chef had combined the ingredients of flour, shortening, baking soda, and salt earlier in the day, letting them sit until he needed to bake a batch of biscuits. All he had to do was measure out enough of these ingredients for a single serving, add milk, then shape and bake. Smith brought the idea back to General Mills where Bisquick was concocted and made "anybody a perfect biscuit maker."

The introduction of Jiffy and Bisquick heralded a new dawn for bakers. These convenience baking products were here to stay, motivating copycats and those in search of easy, delicious bread. In today's burgeoning line of convenience foods, Jiffy remains a popular baking mix, and Chelsea Milling Company is still family owned.

Another product evolving out of the desire for quick baked bread was Brown 'n Serve rolls, which General Mills debuted in 1949. These prebaked rolls and biscuits were stored at room temperature or in the freezer, giving birth to a new convenience food concept. All the home cook had to do was place the partially baked rolls in a preheated oven for a designated time to produce fresh, hot dinner rolls for the family. No mixing. No shaping. No clean up. Only baking was required.

In 1950, a little-known company in the northeast, Ballard & Ballard, was the first on the scene to market raw refrigerated biscuits in a tube package that popped open when the label was removed and the tip of a spoon was pressed against the inner wrap. Intrigued with the concepts of refrigerated dough and packaging technology, Pillsbury purchased the company in 1951.

Three years later, everyone was making quick cinnamon rolls. Seven years later, ten different refrigerated biscuits and roll varieties hit the supermarkets. The busy family cook really had a prepared pantry in the refrigerator. Versatile and delicious, these doughs were at the ready for breakfast, lunch, and dinner every day of the week. The cherubic Pillsbury Doughboy came on the scene in 1965 as a helper, friend, and instructor—roles he maintains to this day.

51 Fast and Fun Packaged Dough Recipes brings the best and most exciting convenience dough recipes to your kitchen. Some of these recipes are riffs on standards, while others are new and worthy of becoming family favorites.

Doughs like refrigerated sweet rolls, canned biscuits, puff pastry, and boxed baking mix produce a collection of savory dishes, to take you from breakfasts to dinner and even dessert. Enjoy practical, delicious, and wholesome foods with recipes like Ham and Cheese Waffles, Beef and Vegetable Dumpling Stew, Mexican Cheese Bread, and Pecan Pie Bars.

Today's home cooks have sophisticated tastes and they understand the importance of bread in a balanced diet. The possibilities are limitless for creating tasty, economical, and convenient meals that look professionally produced. With *51 Fast and Fun Packaged Dough Recipes*, you can prove it is not necessary to be a graduate pastry chef to make some of the best baked items. The secrets are right here in this collection, so start baking!

Tips for Success

1. Keep refrigerated packaged doughs cold. If doughs become warm, they'll be sticky and not respond exactly the way you want them to.

2. Keep boxed baking mix in the refrigerator or freezer—either pour the mix into a labeled airtight container or place the box in a plastic bag. The chill maintains the ingredients at the best possible state and the mix will last longer.

3. Even though the boxed baking mix may be beyond its expiration date, it continues to be good to use for a while. After too long, however, pancakes may flatten and biscuits may not rise much—sure signs a new box is needed.

4. Preheat the oven as directions suggest. The hot oven encourages the most rise in your breads and muffins and crisps up the crusts.

5. Save clean-up time by glossing pans and waffle irons with nonstick cooking spray. This light coating of vegetable oil also speeds up the baking.

6. Use a pastry brush on pans to smooth out and eliminate any foam from nonstick cooking spray.

7. For deep-dish pies, use a roomy pan or dish so your ingredients won't bubble over in the oven. Pyrex dishes are relatively inexpensive, distribute heat evenly, produce pies with golden crusts, and you can see what's going on—whether or not the bottom crust is done—they're predictable and reliable. Emile Henry pie plates from France are made of clay from the Burgundy region of France and have been known for their heat retention and diffusion. Phaltzgraph stoneware and Pampered Chef stoneware produce excellent results as well. If you're in a quandary about your pie plate size, measure across the opening with a ruler.

8. Convenience is the name of the game and the major concept of this book. Refrigerated pie crusts turn out flavorful, flaky, and tender; they're easy to use and quickly adjust their shape over any filling. Follow the directions and the pastry will be just the way you want it.

Although the refrigerated crust is designed for a 9-inch pie pan, it will roll out to a slightly larger size. Use a light touch, rolling from the center out to the edges on a lightly floured surface. It's also a good idea to lightly flour the rolling pin.

9. All of the recipes in this book have short prep times and lend themselves to make-ahead preparations with a few last-minute steps. Spray the baking pans ahead of time. Keep frozen chopped onions on hand. Use your food processor—it's great for chopping celery and carrots.

10. Measure boxed baking mixes by lightly spooning the mix to overflowing into a dry-ingredient measuring cup. Neither sifting nor packing down is required. Level off the excess with the straight edge of a knife.

11. Biscuits require a light touch when kneading, rolling, and shaping. Refrain from mashing down on the dough.

12. Use the biscuit cutter as if you were stamping out biscuits: Cut straight down without twisting the cutter. This technique produces lighter, higher rising biscuits.

13. Yeast dough has a mind of its own. Too much rolling or kneading activity causes the dough to spring back, to retract on itself. This occurs because the gluten has become overactive; at this point it's stretched to its limits. The cure is to lightly flour the dough and let it rest a couple of minutes before proceeding.

14. Spoon all-purpose flour from the sack or a container into the graduated measuring cup. Unless otherwise stated, this is the way recipes using flour and other dry ingredients are constructed. Liquids are measured in glass cups designed with a spout for pouring.

15. Flash freezing is a great way to freeze baked goods for later use. Place the thoroughly cooled items—cookies, scones, cupcakes, muffins, even frosted cakes—on a baking pan and freeze, uncovered, until rock hard. Then place them in an air-tight freezer container, storage bag, or cake saver until needed.

Breakfast

Whether it's a midnight supper with Champagne or a picnic on the beach while watching the sunrise, these breakfasts bring delicious flavors and textures together in a harmonious union. Mixing different ingredients with boxed baking mix gives new flavor to the ordinary waffles. And it's never been easier to put together an impressive dish when using packaged pie crust dough or puff pastry to make an early morning quiche and breakfast tarts. With their wholesome ingredients and beautiful presentation, these dishes will be enjoyed by the whole family.

Ham and Cheese Waffles

These unusual waffles are flavored with ham and cheese. They come out crisp from the iron, but soften nicely within a few minutes. Enjoy them with eggs for breakfast or as an accompaniment with soup.

1. Preheat the waffle iron to manufacturer's specifications. Spray the waffle grids with nonstick cooking spray, if necessary.

2. Whisk together the baking mix, milk, eggs, oil, and butter until smooth. Fold in the cheese and ham.

3. Ladle out the amount of batter recommended by the manufacturer onto the grids, spreading it out with the back of the ladle. Close the lid and bake until steam no longer swirls from the lid and the waffle is golden and crisp, or as per manufacturer's instructions.

4. Remove waffle from the iron and place on a serving dish. Repeat to make remaining waffles, placing on individual dishes; do not stack. Or, if desired, keep them warm in a 200°F oven with the door slightly ajar.

3 cups boxed baking mix
2 cups milk
2 large eggs, slightly beaten
2 tablespoons oil
2 tablespoons unsalted butter, melted
2/3 cup shredded Cheddar cheese (3 ounces)
2/3 cup chopped ham

Cornmeal Waffles

1 1/2 cups self-rising
  cornmeal mix
1/3 cup boxed baking mix
1 tablespoon sugar
1 1/2 cups milk
1 large egg
2 tablespoons canola oil
2 tablespoons unsalted
  butter, melted

An alternative mealtime treat, waffles add an old-fashioned touch that everyone enjoys. These crisp waffles partner well with maple syrup, as well as chili or stew. The oil added to the batter keeps the waffles from sticking to the iron.

1. Preheat the waffle iron to manufacturer's specifications. Spray the waffle grids with nonstick cooking spray, if necessary.

2. Whisk together the cornmeal and baking mixes with the sugar in a large bowl. In a separate bowl, whisk together the milk, egg, oil, and butter. Lightly whisk the wet ingredients into the dry mixture.

3. Ladle the amount of batter recommended by the manufacturer onto the grids, spreading it with the back of the ladle. Close the lid and bake until steam no longer swirls from under the lid and the waffle is golden and crisp, or as per manufacturer's instructions. Serve the waffles immediately.

4. To keep waffles warm and crisp, place them on a hot baking sheet in a preheated 200°F oven with the door slightly ajar. Avoid stacking the waffles.

Chicken and Chile
Quiche Lorraine

Quiche is the classic French baked pie of rich cream and eggs. When it's Quiche Lorraine, you know it contains bacon as well. But quiche can be anything you make it—here it's been given a Mexican touch. Substitute well-drained, chopped marinated artichoke hearts for the chiles or chicken, if you wish.

1. Position the oven rack in the lower third of the oven. Preheat the oven to 375°F.

2. Roll out the pie crust into a 12-inch circle on a lightly floured surface. Line a 10-inch glass pie pan with the crust, easing it in and turning the edges under. Flute the edge of the pie crust by placing your index finger of one hand under the edge of the pastry and placing your thumb and index finger of the other hand on the outside. Pinch the pastry in a V along the edge. Repeat the pinching to reinforcing the shape.

3. Sprinkle the bacon into the crust and top with the chiles, chicken, and 2 cups of the cheese. In a medium bowl whisk the eggs lightly to combine. Add the cream, half-and-half, cayenne pepper, and baking mix whisking until the mixture is smooth.

4. Pull out the oven rack and place the pie on the rack. Slowly pour the egg mixture into the pie pan. Sprinkle the top with the remaining cheese. Gently push the oven rack back into the oven. Bake for 35 to 45 minutes, or until a tester inserted in the center comes out clean.

5. Transfer the quiche to a wire rack and allow it to sit, 5 to 7 minutes. Serve hot or warm with fresh seasonal fruit, like summer melon.

1 refrigerated pie crust (from a 15-ounce box), softened according to package directions

1/2 pound bacon, cooked until crisp, crumbled

1 (4-ounce) can chopped green chiles, drained

1 cup diced cooked plain or Southwestern-seasoned chicken

2 1/4 cups shredded Swiss or Monterey Jack cheese (9 ounces)

3 large eggs

1 cup heavy cream

1/2 cup half-and-half

Dash of cayenne pepper

2 tablespoons boxed baking mix

Canadian Bacon and Potato Bake

2 tablespoons unsalted
   butter
12 slices (about 1 pound)
   Canadian bacon, sliced
   into thin strips
1/3 cup dehydrated chopped
   onion
3 cups frozen hash brown
   potatoes (shredded or
   country style)
3 cups shredded Cheddar
   cheese (12 ounces)
1 cup boxed baking mix
1/4 cup minced fresh parsley
   leaves
2 tablespoons dried chives
1/4 teaspoon black pepper
2 cups whole or 2% milk
4 large eggs, lightly beaten

This layered casserole can be prepared ahead of time, refrigerated, and baked just before serving. Feel free to mix in frozen peas or cooked lima beans, if desired.

1. Position the oven rack in the center of the oven. Preheat oven to 400°F. Coat a 9 x 13-inch baking dish with nonstick cooking spray.

2. Melt the butter in a medium skillet and cook the bacon strips, stirring constantly, until lightly brown around the edges. Combine the bacon strips with the onion, hash browns, and 2 cups cheese, in a large bowl. Place these ingredients in the prepared baking dish.

3. Combine the baking mix with the parsley, chives, and black pepper in the empty bowl. Whisk together the milk and eggs in another bowl. Pour the liquid into the dry ingredients and mix with a fork until thoroughly combined. Pour evenly over the hash brown mixture in the baking dish, tilting the dish to distribute evenly, if necessary.

4. Bake uncovered for 40 minutes. Distribute the remaining cheese over the top. Continue baking a few minutes more, or until the cheese is melted.

5. Allow the casserole to sit about 5 minutes before serving.

Ham and Cheese Free-Form Tart

This attractive ham and cheese tart is the perfect entrée for a brunch when paired with fresh fruit. Or cut the tart into small wedges and serve at room temperature for a picnic lunch.

1. Preheat oven to 375°F. Line a 15 1/2 x 10-inch baking sheet with aluminum foil and coat with nonstick cooking spray. Set aside.

2. Combine the cheese with the ham, mayonnaise, mustard, thyme, lemon juice, and chives in a medium bowl.

3. Lightly dust a work surface area and unfold the sheet of pastry on it. Dust a rolling pin with flour. Roll the pastry to a 16 x 7-inch rectangle. Cut in half lengthwise. Place half the pastry on the prepared sheet. Spread the cheese mixture on the pastry to within 1/2-inch of the edges.

4. Fold the remaining pastry in half. Cut diagonal 1/8-inch-deep slashes through the dough along the folded edge. Unfold the pastry on top of the cheese (the slashes will be positioned down the center of the tart and act as vents as well as decoration). Trim the edges to even, if necessary. Press the edges closed with a fork. Brush the cream over the pastry.

5. Bake for 25 to 35 minutes or until the pastry is golden brown. Remove the tart from the oven and allow it to cool for 5 minutes before serving.

2 cups shredded Monterey Jack or Cheddar cheese (8 ounces)
1 1/2 cups chopped ham
1/2 to 3/4 cup mayonnaise
1 teaspoon dry mustard
1 teaspoon dried thyme
1 teaspoon lemon juice
1 tablespoon snipped fresh chives
1 sheet (from a 17.3-ounce box) frozen puff pastry, thawed
1 tablespoon heavy cream or half-and-half

Appetizers

Appetizers can be served any time of the day. They are finger foods that can carry you through brunch or lunch with ease as well as constitute a light dinner with a salad. Served before a meal, these tasty appetizers stimulate the palate for the entrée pleasures to come or are bite-size treats for the cocktail hour. Prepare some of the following simple appetizers ahead of time and have them handy in the freezer for last-minute guests. Simply flash freeze them uncovered on a baking sheet in the freezer and then store them in airtight freezer bags or containers to avoid freezer burn.

Cheese and Spinach-Stuffed Free-Form Tart

This outstanding recipe goes well with soup or as a special hot sandwich with salad. It is equally delicious whether served as an appetizer hot from the oven or warm at room temperature.

1 (10-ounce) package frozen chopped spinach, thawed, squeezed dry
1 1/2 cups shredded Monterey Jack cheese (6 ounces)
2/3 cup mayonnaise
Pinch of garlic-parsley salt
1 sheet frozen puff pastry (from a 17.3-ounce box), thawed
1 tablespoon heavy cream or half-and-half

1. Preheat oven to 375°F. Line a baking sheet with aluminum foil and coat with nonstick cooking sray. Set aside.

2. Combine the spinach with the cheese, mayonnaise, and garlic-parsley salt in a small bowl.

3. Lightly dust a work surface with flour and unfold the sheet of pastry on it. Dust a rolling pin with flour. Roll the pastry to a 16 x 7-inch rectangle. Cut in half lengthwise. Place half the pastry on the prepared sheet. Spread the cheese mixture to within 1/2-inch of the edges.

4. Fold the remaining pastry in half. Cut diagonal 1/8-inch-deep slashes through the dough along the folded edge. Unfold the pastry on top of the cheese (the slashes will be positioned down the center of the tart and act as vents as well as decoration). Trim the edges to even, if necessary. Press the edges closed with a fork. Brush the cream over the pastry.

5. Bake for 25 to 35 minutes or until the pastry is golden brown. Remove the tart from the oven and allow it to cool for 5 minutes. Cut into large or small wedges, depending on the occasion.

Sausage Balls

1 (1 pound) tube breakfast sausage, hot or mild
4 cups boxed baking mix
4 cups Mexican-style shredded cheese (about 1 pound)
2 tablespoons water
2 teaspoons garlic-pepper salt, or to taste
2 dashes of hot sauce (optional)

These zesty sausage balls are the hit of a party. And since they freeze well, it's a good idea to have a bag of them in the freezer for unexpected guests or late-night snacks. Before freezing, test-bake a ball to see if it comes out round; if it goes flat, add a little more baking mix.

1. Preheat oven to 325°F. Coat a baking sheet with nonstick cooking spray and set aside.

2. Cook the sausage in a large skillet over medium-high heat until no longer pink, 8 to 11 minutes. While cooking, break up the large pieces into crumbles. Drain well and pat off excess fat with paper towels.

3. Combine the remaining ingredients in a large mixing bowl. Add the sausage. Roll into tablespoon-size balls. Place on the baking sheet.

4. Bake the sausage balls for 10 minutes. Roll the balls over, and bake 10 minutes longer or until golden brown. Serve hot with toothpicks.

Mini Cheese Quiches

The most time-consuming part of this recipe is separating the biscuits into layers. The biscuits split more easily if the dough is refrigerator-cold. You can use scraps of dough to patch uneven shells. Serve these little quiches as a pass-around hors d'oeuvre or with soup and salad.

1 (10-count) can refrigerated Flaky Golden Layer biscuits

1/2 cup shredded or grated sharp Swiss or Gruyère cheese (about 2 ounces)

1 large egg, beaten

1/2 cup heavy cream

1 tablespoon dry white wine

1/2 teaspoon lemon-pepper seasoning

1. Preheat oven to 375°F. Butter 24 (about 1 3/4 inches wide) mini muffin cups.

2. Separate each biscuit roll into 2 or 3 layers. Press each portion into the bottom and partly up the sides of a muffin cup to make a shell. Place about 2 teaspoons cheese in each shell.

3. Combine the egg with the cream, wine, and seasoning. Ladle about 1 tablespoonful of the custard over the cheese in each cup. Sprinkle any remaining cheese over the custard.

4. Place the mini quiches in the oven and bake for 20 minutes or until golden. Place the pans on a rack and cool about 5 minutes. Transfer each mini quiche from the muffin pan to the rack to cool completely, or serve warm from the oven in a napkin-lined basket.

Note: You can flash-freeze the cooked quiches. Pack in airtight containers or freezer bags until needed. Reheat frozen quiches on a baking pan in a 375°F oven for 10 to 12 minutes or until defrosted and hot.

Squash Squares

1 cup boxed buttermilk
   baking mix
1/2 cup grated Parmesan
   cheese (about 2 ounces)
4 large eggs, lightly beaten
3 cups thinly sliced zucchini
   or yellow squash, or a
   combination
1/2 cup finely chopped
   green bell pepper
1/2 cup finely chopped
   onion
2 tablespoons chopped fresh
   parsley
1/2 teaspoon Greek
   seasoning
Dash of pepper
1/2 cup light olive or canola
   oil

Welcome the harvest of zucchini and yellow squash from the summer garden by making this tasty treat. Use firm and tender small squash, if possible; mature squash contain a lot of water and large seeds, and have a tough rind.

1. Preheat oven to 350°F. Coat a 9 x 13-inch glass baking dish with nonstick cooking spray.

2. Combine the baking mix, cheese, eggs, squash, pepper, onion, parsley, Greek seasoning, black pepper, and oil in a large bowl until well blended. Transfer the mixture into the prepared pan, smoothing the top. Bake 25 to 30 minutes or until golden brown and a tester inserted in the center comes out clean.

3. Allow the dish to cool on a wire rack. Cut into bite-size pieces and serve.

Chinese Dumplings

These are as much fun to make, as they are to eat. Using regular tube sausage for the filling and refrigerated buttermilk biscuits for the dumplings, these delights put on a show turning over as they poach in water. Serve as a hors d'oeuvre, a snack, or in vegetable soups, where they cook in the broth.

1. Combine the sausage, scallion, and egg white in a small bowl. Shape 20 teaspoon-size balls of the mixture and set aside on a piece of wax paper.

2. Remove the biscuits from the can and line them up on a sheet of aluminum foil. Cut each biscuit in half. Place 1 sausage ball on each biscuit half and shape the dough to fit over the ball until covered. Pinch closed, making a top knot on the dumpling; set aside.

3. Bring a large pot of water to a boil. Place half the dumplings in the water and poach for 5 to 7 minutes, nudging them to turn over from time to time. Remove the dumplings with a slotted spoon and drain in a colander. Cook the remaining dumplings in the boiling water and drain.

4. Warm the oil with the butter in a large skillet over medium heat. When the sizzle subsides, add a few dumplings and lightly brown on all sides. Drain on paper towels. Keep warm on a heated platter or in a warm oven. Continue browning all the dumplings.

5. Make the dipping sauce by combining the soy sauce, scallion, and sesame oil in a bowl, mixing well. Serve dumplings with toothpicks and the dipping sauce.

Dumplings:
1/2 pound (8 ounces) seasoned tube sausage
1 scallion, trimmed, thinly sliced
1 large egg white
1 (10-count) can refrigerated Buttermilk biscuits
2 tablespoons olive oil
2 tablespoons unsalted butter

Dipping Sauce:
3 tablespoons soy sauce
1 scallion, trimmed, finely minced
Few drops of roasted sesame oil

Sandwiches

The simple design of a sandwich—a filling between two pieces of bread—probably developed during the evolution of Mediterranean unleavened breads, such as matzo, one of the world's seminal breads. Sandwiches came into their own in the eighteenth century when John Montague, the fourth Earl of Sandwich, refused to leave a gambling table and asked for sustenance. His chef prepared a snack by enclosing a thin layer of a savory mixture between two pieces of buttered bread that the Earl ate out of hand, and the sandwich was born. The French grabbed on to this idea while the English miniaturized it with tea sandwiches, and up north, the Scandinavians had a jump on everyone—they had been feasting on open-faced sandwiches for generations. Today, the variations on sandwiches are endless and eminently delicious.

With cooked Italian sausages stashed in the freezer and cans of breadsticks in the fridge, this riff on pigs in a blanket is a quick dish. Supermarkets stock frozen cooked sausages and bratwurst in the freezer section near the meat department.

6 to 12 frozen cooked Italian sausages or bratwurst
1 (11-ounce) can refrigerated Soft Breadsticks
Mustard and ketchup, for dipping

1. Position the oven rack below center and preheat the oven to 375°F. Line a baking sheet with aluminum foil. Lightly coat the foil with nonstick cooking spray and set aside.

2. Rinse ice particles from the sausages under cold running water. Blot the sausages with paper towels.

3. Place the dough on a work surface and separate into 12 strips. Wrap each sausage with a breadstick strip starting at one end and wrapping the dough diagonally to the opposite end. Arrange the wrapped sausages on the prepared pan with about a 2-inch space between each, and with dough ends facing down on the pan.

4. Bake 15 to 20 minutes or until the sarapes are golden brown. Serve one or two sausages hot from the oven to each person with mustard and ketchup on the side.

Pizza Pronto

1 (8-count) can refrigerated Grands! Buttermilk biscuits
1 (8-ounce) jar favorite pizza sauce
1/2 teaspoon Italian seasoning
32 thin slices pepperoni
1 to 2 cups shredded mozzarella cheese (4 to 8 ounces)

There's nothing quite as handy as individual pizzas when you are in a hurry. Keep your favorite pizza ingredients in the pantry and refrigerator, or prepare these ahead of time, flash freeze them uncovered, and then layer them in a freezer container until needed.

1. Preheat oven to 375°F. Line 2 baking sheets with aluminum foil. Coat the foil with nonstick cooking spray and set aside.

2. Remove the biscuits from the can and place them on a work surface. Separate the biscuits and divide each biscuit into two halves. Line the baking sheets with the biscuit halves. Bake for about 5 minutes.

3. Blend the pizza sauce and Italian seasoning in a bowl. Spread each biscuit half with some sauce, add 2 slices of pepperoni, and top with a sprinkling of cheese.

4. Bake for 15 to 20 minutes or until the biscuits are browned and the cheese is bubbly. Serve hot from the oven.

Salmon with Dill and Cream Cheese Focaccia

This is where heaven and earth meet—on home-baked focaccia bread topped with smoked salmon, dill-seasoned cream cheese, and a sprinkling of capers. It's an elegant and totally delicious combination worthy of a fine Pinot Noir or Pinot Grigio served in your best glasses. Perfect served as an appetizer, for Sunday breakfast, or as the accompaniment to a salad for a light meal.

2 to 4 tablespoons olive oil
1 (13.8-ounce) can classic pizza crust
All-purpose flour
1/4 teaspoon salt
1/4 teaspoon pepper
1 (8-ounce) container whipped cream cheese
1 1/2 teaspoons dried dill leaves or 1 tablespoon fresh
4 scallions, ends trimmed, thinly sliced
6 ounces thinly sliced smoked salmon
1/4 cup drained capers, rinsed

1. Position a rack in the lower third of the oven and preheat to 400°F. Line a 12-inch pizza pan or 15 1/2 x 12-inch baking sheet with aluminum foil and brush with olive oil.

2. Place the pizza dough on a lightly floured work surface and cut in half. Flatten one tubular piece of dough, sprinkle with a little flour, and roll out, stretching the dough if necessary, to a rectangle measuring roughly 9 x 7 inches. Place the dough on the prepared pan. Repeat the same technique with the other half of dough.

3. Dimple each piece of dough with your fingertips and brush with 2 tablespoons olive oil. Sprinkle with a little salt and pepper. Reduce the oven temperature to 375°F. Bake for 10 to 11 minutes, or until golden blisters appear, the bottom is crisp, and the surface springs back when pressed. Allow to cool for 15 minutes in the pan.

4. Combine the cream cheese, dill, and the white parts of the scallions. Spread the cheese generously on the warm bread. Top with pieces of smoked salmon. Distribute the remaining scallions and capers over the top. Slice the focaccia into wedges as desired and serve.

Hot Barbecue Biscuits

1 (8-count) can refrigerated buttermilk Grands! Flaky Layers

1 pound container of favorite prepared barbecued meat

1 pound deli cole slaw, to serve

Barbecue doesn't come much easier than this. Pile your favorite commercially prepared seasoned pork, chicken, or beef on grand-sized biscuits and bake them in your home oven until golden brown. Supermarkets stock various brands of prepared barbecue in their meat and deli departments.

1. Preheat oven to 350°F. Line a baking sheet with aluminum foil. Coat the foil with nonstick cooking spray and set aside.

2. Remove the biscuits from the can onto a work surface. Separate the biscuits and divide into two halves. Line the baking sheet with half of the biscuit halves.

3. Mound 2 to 3 tablespoons of the prepared barbecued meat on each biscuit half. Place the other biscuit halves on top and gently press down.

4. Bake for 13 minutes or until the biscuits are nicely browned. Remove from the oven and eat hot with cole slaw.

Tuna Melts

*It's great to have some packaged dough on hand in the refrigerator.
These tuna melts make a delicious and nutritious lunch for the whole family,
and can be assembled in no time with packaged dough. If you want to
stretch the recipe, make 16 open-faced melts.*

2 (6-ounce) cans tuna in water, well drained
1/4 cup mayonnaise
Pinch of salt
Pinch of black pepper
1 (8-count) can refrigerated Buttermilk Grands! Flaky Layers
8 or 16 slices American cheese (or 2/3 cup shredded Cheddar cheese)

1. Preheat oven to 350°F. Line a baking sheet with aluminum foil. Coat the foil with nonstick cooking spray and set aside.

2. Combine the tuna, mayonnaise, salt, and pepper in a medium bowl.

3. Remove the biscuits from the can onto a work surface. Separate the biscuits and divide into two halves. Line the baking sheets with half of the biscuit halves.

4. Mound 2 to 3 tablespoons of tuna mix on each biscuit. Place 2 slices (1 slice per half if you make open-faced sandwiches) of cheese over the tuna. Place the biscuit tops on the cheese and gently press down.

5. Bake for 13 minutes or until the biscuits are nicely browned. Remove from the oven and eat hot.

Cheese-Filled Swirls

10 thin slices pepperoni or
chorizo sausage

2 cups shredded Mexican-
style cheese (8-ounces)

1 teaspoon minced chives

1 teaspoon diced chiles,
drained, rinsed

3 tablespoons mayonnaise

1 (8-ounce) can refrigerated
Original Crescent rolls

Salsa, to serve

Sour cream, to serve

Tender, light rolls with a Mexican-inspired filling of mixed cheeses, and diced chiles make a tasty meal on the go as well as a partner to soups and salads. Cutting the rolls with plain dental floss using a sawing motion eliminates squashed rolls.

1. Preheat oven to 375°F. Line a baking sheet with aluminum foil. Coat the foil with nonstick cooking spray and set aside.

2. Combine the pepperoni, cheese, chives, chiles, and mayonnaise in a food processor. Pulse on/off several times to mix the ingredients.

3. Unroll the dough on a lightly floured surface. Pinch the perforations to seal the dough.

4. Spread the filling mixture over the dough to within 1/4-inch of the edges. Roll from the long end (as if making a jelly roll) until one long cylinder forms. Pinch the edges to seal.

5. Cut into 8 rolls using either a knife or plain dental floss. Place the rolls on the prepared baking sheet, shaping them into a round, if necessary.

6. Bake for 15 minutes or until golden brown. Remove from the sheet immediately and place on a serving dish. Serve piping hot with salsa and sour cream.

Cheese and Spinach-Stuffed Loaf

Seasoned spinach and cheese spread on flaky crescent roll dough bakes to golden perfection. Accompanied by a salad of orange slices and romaine lettuce, this dish makes a lovely luncheon treat. A real plus is this loaf can be prepared ahead of time and refrigerated until needed.

1 (10-ounce) package frozen chopped spinach, thawed, squeezed of excess water
1 cup shredded mozzarella or Monterey Jack cheese (about 4 ounces)
1/3 cup mayonnaise
Pinch of garlic-parsley powder
2 (8-ounce) cans refrigerated Original Crescent rolls
1 tablespoon butter, melted

1. Preheat oven to 375°F. Line a baking sheet with aluminum foil. Coat the foil with nonstick cooking spray and set aside.

2. Combine the spinach with half of the cheese, mayonnaise, and seasoning in a small bowl.

3. Unroll 1 can of dough on the baking sheet. Seal perforations by pinching openings together. On both long sides of the dough, cut diagonal strips 3 inches in length and 3 inches apart.

4. Spread half the filling down the middle of the dough. Lift the strips of dough across the filling to meet in the center and lay one on the other. Turn the short ends of the dough under and seal by crimping with a fork. Set aside.

5. Repeat the steps with the second can of dough. Brush melted butter over the tops of both loaves. Bake for 25 to 30 minutes or until golden brown. Allow loaves to sit for 5 minutes before you slice the loaves and serve.

Four Seasons Pizza

1 (13.8-ounce) can
   refrigerated pizza crust
1 (10.6-ounce) can
   refrigerated plain
   breadsticks
4 cheese sticks, split
   lengthwise (any kind of
   cheese works)
1/4 pound thinly sliced
   prosciutto or deli ham
1 cup shredded mozzarella
   cheese (about 4 ounces)
1 cup thinly sliced button
   mushrooms
1 or 2 garlic cloves, minced
3/4 cup chopped ripe
   tomatoes or tomatoes
   mixed with a little tomato
   sauce
1 cup chopped marinated
   artichoke hearts, drained
   and patted dry

2 tablespoons grated
   Parmesan cheese
Olive oil
1 tablespoon thinly sliced
   fresh basil leaves, or 1 1/2
   teaspoons dried

This beautiful pizza, actually an open-faced sandwich, is so named because it is divided into four quarters, with each section representing a different season. Twisted breadsticks separate the different toppings. Use toppings to suit your preferences and the season: shellfish, wild mushrooms, fresh herbs, garden tomatoes, crushed meatballs, and grilled vegetables.

1. Position the oven rack in the lower third of the oven. Preheat oven to 400°F. Lightly oil a 12-inch pizza pan.

2. Shape the pizza dough into a ball and place it on the pan. Begin pushing the dough from the center out to the edges until it fills the pan. (If there are tears or holes, use leftover breadstick dough as the patch.)

3. Twist two breadsticks together and place across the dough at right angles to divide the dough into 4 quarters. Snip off the excess with scissors.

4. Roll half a cheese stick in each piece of leftover breadstick dough to encase it. Place it seam side down around the edge of the pizza dough.

5. Bake the pizza dough for 6 to 8 minutes, then remove it from the oven.

6. Sprinkle the ham and a little mozzarella on one fourth of the pizza, sliced mushrooms mixed with garlic on the second quadrant, chopped tomatoes mixed with basil and the remaining mozzarella on the third, and the chopped artichoke hearts sprinkled with Parmesan cheese on the final quadrant. Drizzle all of the ingredients with a little olive oil.

7. Bake for 15 to 20 minutes, or until the crust and breadsticks are golden brown and the cheese is melted and bubbly. Serve hot.

Entrées

Packaged dough such as crescent rolls, puff pastry, and boxed baking mix help home cooks put wholesome, savory dishes on the table. Great one-dish meals are fabulous for the whole family or for when you have guests, especially when the components are prepared in advance and the final assembly or baking takes place while you're doing something else—like enjoying your own party! These basic recipes allow the cook to be inventive with a variety of ingredients, so go ahead and make these suggestions a springboard for your own creativity. Maintaining an inventory of favorite packaged dough in the refrigerator, along with stocking frequently used pantry items, will give you entrée options galore.

Spinach, Ham, and Cheese Braid

A lovely and delicious lunch or dinner course, this delectable braid enfolds an array of harmonizing flavors, which blend into the melted cheese. Accompany this with a nice tossed salad and fruit for dessert.

1. Positioin the oven rack in the lower third of the oven. Preheat oven to 375°F. Cover a 17 x 14-inch baking pan with aluminum foil. Coat the foil with nonstick cooking spray and set aside.

2. Combine the spinach with the garlic, 1/2 cup of the mayonnaise, the cheese, Italian seasoning, and chives in a large bowl.

3. Unroll the dough in the center of the baking pan. Seal the perforations by pinching; smooth the dough out by rolling with a rolling pin or a smooth glass or jar. Use a ruler to mark a 6-inch area down the center for the filling. On both long sides of the dough, cut diagonal strips 3 inches in length and 3 inches apart.

4. Spread the remaining 1 tablespoon mayonnaise and the mustard down the center of the dough in the marked area. Place the ham slices overlapping down the center of the dough. Spread the spinach mixture over the ham, smoothing it to fill the marked area.

5. Lift the strips of dough across the filling to meet in the center, laying one on the other. Turn the short ends of the dough under and seal by crimping with a fork.

6. Bake for 30 to 35 minutes, or until the braid is golden brown and the cheese is bubbly. Allow the braid to sit for 10 minutes, then slice on the diagonal and serve.

1 (10-ounce) package frozen chopped spinach, thawed, squeezed of excess water

1 garlic clove, finely minced or pressed

1/2 cup plus 1 tablespoon mayonnaise

1 1/2 cups shredded Italian 4-cheese blend or mozzarella cheese (about 6 ounces)

1 teaspoon Italian seasoning

1 tablespoon chopped fresh or dried chives

1 (10.1-ounce) can refrigerated Big & Flaky Crescent rolls

1 tablespoon Dijon mustard

8 pieces deli ham, thinly sliced

Cornmeal-Topped Beef with Sausage and Cheese Casserole

Filling:
- 2 tablespoons olive oil
- 1 pound ground beef
- 1 large onion, chopped
- 2 teaspoons minced garlic
- 1/2 cup salsa of choice
- 1 (8-ounce) can tomato sauce
- 1 (14.5-ounce) can diced tomatoes
- 3 frozen Italian sausages, cooked, cut in thirds
- 1/2 teaspoon ground cumin
- 1 teaspoon chili powder
- 1/2 teaspoon dried Mexican oregano
- 2 cups shredded Mexican-style cheese blend (about 8 ounces)

Assemble this recipe quickly for a satisfying dinner during the week or on Sunday evening. For those who enjoy a little extra heat, fold a can of drained chopped jalapeño chili peppers into either the filling or topping.

Topping:
- 2 large eggs
- 1 cup whole or 2% milk
- 1/2 cup boxed baking mix
- 1/4 cup self-rising cornmeal mix
- 1 1/2 teaspoon snipped chives
- 1 teaspoon chopped fresh parsley

1. Preheat oven to 400°F. Coat a 10-inch deep-dish pie pan or a 2 1/2-quart oval baking dish with nonstick cooking spray.

2. Warm the oil in a large skillet and brown the beef with the onion and garlic until the meat is no longer pink, 7 to 10 minutes. Stir to break up the large pieces. Drain the excess fat.

3. Return the skillet to the heat and stir in the salsa, tomato sauce, tomatoes, sausage, cumin, chili powder, and oregano. Bring to a boil, lower the heat, and cook 10 minutes, stirring occasionally.

4. Combine the eggs with the milk in a 1-quart measuring cup. Combine the baking mix and cornmeal mix with the chives and parsley in a separate large bowl. Pour the egg mixture into the dry ingredients and stir to mix.

5. Transfer the meat mixture to the baking dish. Distribute the cheese over the meat. Spoon the topping over the cheese, smoothing to cover the ingredients.

6. Bake for 30 minutes, or until bubbling hot. Allow the dish sit for several minutes before serving.

Salmon and Mushroom Deep-Dish Pie

You won't have to fish for compliments when you serve this savory pie filled with dill-seasoned mushroom sauce and salmon. Premium pink salmon comes in vacuum-packed pouches and requires only flaking into pieces—without draining.

2 tablespoons unsalted butter

1 tablespoon olive oil

1 (8-ounce) box fresh button mushrooms, sliced, rinsed, patted dry, or 1 (8-ounce) jar, well drained

3 tablespoons all-purpose flour

1 1/2 cups whole or 2% milk

2 vegetable or chicken bouillon cubes, crushed

1 tablespoon dehydrated minced onion

1 teaspoon dried dill

1 teaspoon chopped fresh parsley

1 refrigerated pie crust (from a 15-ounce box), softened according to package directions

2 (7.1-ounce) packages vacuum-packed pink salmon (skinless and boneless), or 1 (16-ounce) can pink salmon, drained well, skin and bones removed

1. Position the rack in the lower third of the oven. Preheat oven to 375°F. Coat a 9- or 10-inch deep-dish pie pan with nonstick cooking spray and set aside.

2. Melt the butter with the oil in a large skillet. Add the mushrooms and cook over medium-high heat until beginning to brown, 5 to 7 minutes. Sprinkle with the flour, and cook, stirring, over medium-low heat for 2 minutes. Gradually add the milk, stirring constantly. Bring the mixture to a low boil; add the bouillon cubes, onion, dill, and parsley. Cook for 2 to 3 minutes, then remove the mushroom sauce from the heat.

3. Unfold the pie crust according to the package directions on a lightly floured surface. Roll the dough into a 12-inch circle. Fold the dough in half and in half again, to make quarters. Make small diagonal cuts in the folds about 1/4-inch apart.

4. Transfer the mushroom sauce to the pie pan. Add the salmon, leaving as many chunks as possible.

5. Unfold the pie crust over the salmon mixture. Fold and roll the overhanging pastry evenly on the rim of the pie pan. Flute the edges of the pie crust by placing your index finger of one hand under the edge of the pastry and placing your thumb and index finger of the other hand on the outside. Pinch the pastry into a V along the edge. Repeat the pinching to reinforce the shape.

6. Bake for 35 to 40 minutes, or until the crust is golden brown and the filling is bubbly. Transfer the pie to a cooling rack. Allow to sit for 10 minutes, then cut into wedges and serve.

Oven-Fried Chicken Fingers

2 tablespoons unsalted
  butter
2 tablespoons canola oil
1 1/2 cups boxed baking mix
2 teaspoons paprika
1 teaspoon salt
1/2 teaspoon black pepper
1 1/3 cups buttermilk
1 1/2 to 2 pounds chicken
  filets or tenders, patted
  dry

*Hardly a potluck picnic goes by without these delectable fried chicken fingers
making an appearance. This casual fare is popular with everyone, even the cook
because after the chicken is floured, the oven does the cooking. Chicken filets or
tenders are the small slender cut from the underside of a chicken breast—there
is no waste only tender meat. For a family meal, pair these with baked
beans, coleslaw, and shortcake for dessert.*

1. Preheat oven to 400°F. Line a 10 x 15-inch baking pan with sides, such as a jelly roll
pan or broiler pan, with aluminum foil.

2. Place the butter and oil in the baking pan, put in the oven, and allow the butter to
melt.

3. Combine the baking mix, paprika, salt, and pepper on a large piece of aluminum
foil. Pour the buttermilk into a shallow bowl. Dip each chicken filet or tender into the
buttermilk, and then roll in the coating. Set aside the floured chicken filet on wax paper
or foil lined platter.

4. Remove the pan from the oven. Place the floured filets, rounded side down in the hot
butter and oil. Return the pan to the oven.

5. Bake for 20 minutes. Remove the pan from the oven. Turn the chicken over and
bake 15 minutes longer, or until the chicken is golden brown. Drain on paper towels,
if necessary. Serve hot or refrigerate for later use.

Hot Chicken Salad and Rolls

This super-easy combination goes together quickly and is great for a large group. Use a rotisserie chicken or turkey from the supermarket to make preparation even easier. Prepare this dish ahead of time, cover, refrigerate, and relax before company arrives; just add 10 to 15 minutes baking time to the chilled dish.

1. Preheat oven to 375°F. Coat a 9 x 13-inch or 3-quart baking dish with nonstick cooking spray and set aside.

2. Combine the mayonnaise, sour cream, soup, pimentos, lemon juice, and onion in a large bowl. Stir in the chicken, celery, and almonds, if using; mix lightly. Transfer the mixture to the prepared baking dish. Sprinkle with the cheese.

3. Remove the tube of crescent roll dough from the can but do not separate. Cut the roll of dough in half; cut the halves in half again to make 4 rolls and cut each roll in half again to make 8 rolls. Cut each of the 8 rolls in half so you end up with a total of 16 half rolls. Arrange the halves, cut side down and sides touching, along the edge of the filling.

4. Bake for 25 minutes or until the ingredients are bubbling up and the bread topping is golden brown. Serve piping hot.

1 cup mayonnaise
1/2 cup sour cream
1 (10 3/4-ounce) can cream of chicken soup
1 (2-ounce) jar pimentos, well drained
2 tablespoons lemon juice
1 tablespoon grated onion
4 cups chopped cooked chicken
3 cups thinly sliced celery
1 cup slivered almonds (optional)
1 cup grated sharp Cheddar cheese (about 4 ounces)
1 (8-ounce) can refrigerated Original Crescent rolls

Creamy Herb Chicken and Broccoli Casserole with Biscuits

3 teaspoons dried Italian
seasoning
1/4 teaspoon salt
Pinch of black pepper
1/2 teaspoon sweet paprika
1 1/2 pounds chicken
breasts, boneless and
skinless
1 cup evaporated milk or
half-and-half
2 tablespoons all-purpose
flour
1 garlic clove, minced
3/4 to 1 cup shredded Swiss
cheese (3 to 4 ounces)
1/4 cup grated Parmesan
cheese (one ounce)
2 (10-ounce) packages
frozen broccoli florets or
cuts, thawed, rinsed, and
drained

This casserole is an easy recipe that combines chicken and broccoli in a smooth cheese sauce. Turkey makes the perfect alternative to the chicken.

2 to 3 tablespoons unsalted
butter
1 (10-count) can
refrigerated Golden
Layers Buttermilk biscuits

1. Preheat oven to 350°F. Coat a 9 x 13-inch baking dish with nonstick cooking spray and set aside.

2. Combine 2 teaspoons of the Italian seasoning, salt, pepper, and paprika. Place the chicken breasts on wax paper and lightly sprinkle the seasoning mix on both sides. Cover the chicken with another piece of wax paper and gently pound to an even thinness. Slice into bite-size pieces or slender strips. Place on a dish and refrigerate until needed.

3. Whisk 1/4 cup of the evaporated milk with the flour and minced garlic in a small saucepan. Whisk in the remaining 3/4 cup milk; add the remaining Italian seasoning. Cook the mixture over moderate heat while stirring until the mixture thickens and comes to a boil. Remove the pan from the heat and stir in the Swiss cheese, reserving 4 tablespoons.

4. Combine the remaining 4 tablespoons cheese with the Parmesan cheese in a small bowl and set aside.

5. Pour 1/3 cup of the cheese sauce on the bottom of the prepared baking dish, tilting to distribute it evenly. Place the broccoli over the sauce.

6. Melt the butter over medium heat in a large skillet and sauté the chicken, turning the pieces until lightly browned. Arrange the pieces over the broccoli as they are cooked. Pour the remaining cheese sauce over the chicken. Sprinkle with the reserved cheese mixture.

7. Separate the biscuits and cut each in half. Arrange the biscuit halves, cut side down and sides touching, around the edge of the filling.

8. Bake for 20 to 30 minutes or until the biscuits are golden brown and the filling is bubbling. Allow the dish to cool 5 to 10 minutes before using a spoon to serve individual portions.

Chili Cobbler

Chili:

3 tablespoons olive oil
1 large onion, minced
2 garlic cloves, minced
**1 1/2 to 2 pounds ground
  beef**
2 tablespoons chili powder
1 teaspoon ground cumin
Pinch of cayenne pepper
**1 teaspoon dried Mexican
  oregano**
1 cup water
**2 (15-ounce) cans tomato
  sauce**
**1 (14.5-ounce) can Mexican-
  style stewed tomatoes,
  with juice**
**1 or 2 (1-pound each) cans
  red kidney beans, rinsed,
  drained**

*This recipe boasts a cornmeal crust which adds textural contrast and makes it a
satisfying one-dish meal. Prepare the chili a few days in advance, warm it before
adding the crust, and then bake these dynamic partners together. Ladle the chili over
cornmeal waffles (see page 12) for an equally delicious dish.*

Topping:

1 1/2 cups boxed baking mix
**1 1/4 cups self-rising
  cornmeal mix**
**1 tablespoon chopped fresh
  cilantro**
1 tablespoon snipped chives
1/2 teaspoon black pepper
**2 to 2 1/4 cups whole or 2%
  milk**
3 tablespoons olive oil
3 large eggs, lightly beaten

1. Warm the oil in a large skillet and cook the onion and garlic until softened, about 11 minutes. Add the beef and cook until no longer pink, 11 to 12 minutes, breaking up the large pieces as the meat cooks. Drain off the excess fat.

2. Return the ingredients to the skillet. Stir in the chili powder, cumin, cayenne, and oregano. Cook over medium-low heat, stirring so the spices don't burn, for about 2 minutes. Pour in the water, tomato sauce, stewed tomatoes, and beans. Stir and cook while bringing to a boil. Reduce the heat to medium-low and cook for about 1 hour, partially covered and stirring occasionally.

3. Preheat oven to 375°F. Coat a 9 x 13-inch baking dish with nonstick cooking spray and set aside.

4. In a large bowl, combine the baking mix, cornmeal mix, cilantro, chives, pepper, milk, olive oil, and eggs and wisk until the batter is thick and well blended.

5. Transfer the chili to the prepared dish. Drop the topping ingredients onto the chili by tablespoonfuls. Don't spread the dough; you want a rough topping.

6. Bake the cobbler for 30 minutes or until the topping is golden brown and a tester inserted in several places in the topping, comes out clean. Allow the casserole to sit about 10 minutes before serving.

Spinach and Cheese Pie

1 (15-ounce) container
whole milk ricotta cheese

1 (10-ounce) package frozen
chopped spinach, thawed,
squeezed dry

4 large eggs, slightly beaten

2 scallions, ends trimmed,
thinly sliced

1/4 cup grated Parmesan
cheese

1/4 pound feta cheese,
crumbled (about 1 cup)

2 teaspoons chopped fresh
dill, or 1 teaspoon dried

1 tablespoon chopped fresh
parsley leaves

6 tablespoons (3/4 stick)
unsalted butter, melted

4 tablespoons olive oil

1 pound phyllo dough,
thawed if frozen

1/4 cup club soda

This Greek-style spinach pie has a filling of herb-seasoned ricotta, feta, and Parmesan cheeses encased in paper-thin phyllo sheets. Phyllo's reputation for being difficult to use isn't true as long as the pastry sheets are kept under a damp towel to prevent drying. Supermarkets sell phyllo frozen in one-pound boxes, and it's best to defrost it overnight in the refrigerator.

1. Preheat oven to 375°F. Coat a 9 x 13-inch baking dish with nonstick cooking spray and set aside.

2. Combine the ricotta, spinach, eggs, scallions, Parmesan cheese, feta cheese, dill, and parsley in a large bowl. Stir and fold the ingredients to mix thoroughly.

3. Combine the butter with the olive oil in a small bowl and set aside.

4. Remove the phyllo from the box and place the stack of dough on a work surface lightly dusted with flour and cover with a damp paper towel.

5. Line the bottom of the prepared baking dish with 8 sheets of phyllo dough, brushing each sheet with a little of the butter and oil combination.

6. Stir the cheese mixture up from the bottom to re-mix. Transfer the mixture to the pastry-lined dish, spreading it evenly from edge to edge. Top the cheese mixture with 6 of the remaining phyllo sheets, brushing each sheet and the top with the butter and oil combination.

7. Make 12 to 15 small slits in the top of the pie with the tip of a sharp knife. Sprinkle the soda water lightly over the top.

8. Butter the 3 remaining sheets of phyllo and bunch them into a ball. Place the ball in the center of the pie for decoration and sprinkle with a little club soda.

9. Bake for 45 to 60 minutes or until the top is golden brown, the filling is set, and a toothpick inserted in the center of the pie comes out clean. Allow the pie to sit for 10 minutes before cutting into portions.

Chicken and Vegetable Deep-Dish Pie

5 tablespoons unsalted butter
1/3 cup finely chopped onion
1/2 cup thinly sliced celery
1/4 cup boxed baking mix
2 1/2 cups chicken broth
1 cup plus 1 tablespoon heavy cream
1 chicken bouillon cube, crushed
2 1/2 cups chopped cooked chicken
1 (10-ounce) package frozen peas and carrots, thawed, and drained
1/4 teaspoon black pepper
2 tablespoons minced fresh parsley
1 refrigerated pie crust (from a 15-ounce box), softened according to package directions

This deep-dish pie offers a heavy dose of creamy chicken filling studded with vegetables. Featured on the cover of this cookbook, it's the perfect dish for a potluck. Try turkey leftovers in this recipe after Thanksgiving.

1. Preheat oven to 400°F. Coat the rim and sides of a 10-inch pie pan with nonstick cooking spray and set aside.

2. Melt the butter in a large, deep skillet over medium heat. Add the onion and celery, and cook until the vegetables soften, 5 to 7 minutes. Stir in the baking mix gradually until absorbed, about 1 minute. Add the broth, 1 cup of the cream, and the crushed bouillon cube while stirring. Bring to a boil, stirring constantly, and cook for 2 minutes or until the mixture thickens.

3. Add the chicken, peas and carrots, pepper, and parsley to the cream sauce. Stir well, then spoon the mixture into the prepared pie pan.

4. Unfold the pie crust on a work surface and roll out to an 11-inch circle. Fold the crust in half and in half again to make quarters. At the point, cut out a 1 3/4- to 1-inch circle and discard; this vent in the center will allow steam to escape while the pastry bakes. Gently unfold the dough over the filling. Tuck the pastry down along the edges of the pie pan. Brush the pastry with the remaining 1 tablespoon of cream.

5. Bake for 35 to 40 minutes, or until the crust is golden brown and juices bubble up through the center vent. Allow the pie to sit for 10 minutes before serving.

Beef and Vegetable Dumpling Stew

Serves 8 to 10

This homespun stew of beef and vegetables is even more of a comfort food with these chive-seasoned dumplings. Instant flour is a finely milled quick-dissolving flour found in the baking section of supermarkets, near the all-purpose flour.

1. Place the meat, bouillon cubes, and water in a 6- to 8-quart stew pot or Dutch oven. Bring to a boil. Reduce the heat to medium and cook 30 minutes. Stir occasionally to make sure the bouillon cubes get dissolved.

2. Add the carrots, onions, paprika, and bay leaf; stir to combine. Bring to a boil over medium high heat. Reduce the heat to medium-low and simmer 2 hours, covered. Add the beans, mushrooms, and peas. Cook 30 to 45 minutes or until all the meat is tender. Dissolve the instant flour into the 1/3 cup water and stir into the hot stew until incorporated. Stir and keep the stew bubbling over medium-low heat.

3. Combine the baking mix with the chives in a medium mixing bowl. Stir in the milk until a soft dough forms.

4. Scoop up a teaspoonful of dumpling dough and use another teaspoon to push it off into the bubbling stew. Continue this until you use up all the dough. Reduce the heat to medium low and cook uncovered for 10 minutes. Cover and cook for 10 minutes longer, or until a tester inserted in the center of a few dumplings comes out clean.

5. Remove the bay leaf. Ladle the stew and dumplings into large soup bowls and serve.

Stew:

3 pounds boneless stew meat or chuck, cut into 1 1/2-inch cubes
6 beef bouillon cubes
6 cups cold water
8 large carrots, cut into 2-inch lengths
3 medium onions, quartered
1 teaspoon sweet paprika
1 bay leaf
2 cups frozen green beans
8 ounces button mushrooms, sliced
2 cups frozen peas
3 tablespoons instant flour
1/3 cup water

Dumplings:

2 cups boxed baking mix
1 tablespoon snipped fresh or dried chives
2/3 cup milk

Turkey and Ham Pie with Biscuits

3 chicken bouillon cubes
2 cups boiling water
4 tablespoons (1/2 stick) unsalted butter
1 tablespoon dehydrated minced onion
1/2 teaspoon garlic salt
1/2 teaspoon sweet paprika
1/4 teaspoon black pepper
1/4 cup all-purpose flour
2 cups chopped turkey
1 cup chopped ham
2 to 3 cups frozen mixed vegetables of choice
1 tablespoon minced fresh parsley leaves
1 (8-ounce) can refrigerated Original Crescent rolls

Prepare this tasty dish during the holidays when these ingredients are plentiful. The halved crescent rolls give an elegant look to the casserole.

1. Preheat oven to 400°F. Coat a 9 x 13-inch baking dish with nonstick cooking spray and set aside.

2. Dissolve the bouillon cubes in the boiling water and set aside.

3. Melt the butter in a skillet over moderate heat. Stir in the onion, garlic salt, paprika, and pepper. Cook while stirring to combine. Add the flour and stir to blend. Add the bouillon water and stir until the sauce thickens and bubbles. Stir in the turkey, ham, and vegetables and cook over medium-high heat until the mixture is hot and begins bubbling. Remove the skillet from the heat and stir in the parsley. Transfer the mixture to the prepared baking dish.

4. Remove the tube of crescent roll dough from the can but do not separate. Cut the roll of dough in half, then cut the halves in half again to make 4 rolls. Cut each roll in half to make 8 smaller rolls. Cut each of the 8 rolls in half so you have a total of 16 pieces of dough. Arrange the halves cut side down and sides touching along the edge of the filling.

5. Bake for 15 to 20 minutes or until the biscuits on top are golden brown and the filling is bubbling up in the center. Allow the dish to cool 5 to 10 minutes before using a spoon to serve individual portions.

Sunday Chicken Casserole with Puff Pastry Crust

Creamy chicken and vegetables are the hearty, homespun contents beneath the sophisticated puff pastry crust. "Herbes de Provence" combines several aromatic herbs used in the south of France, such as basil, summer savory, thyme, marjoram, bay leaf, rosemary, and usually lavender. Supermarkets stock this herb with the other spices.

1. Position the oven rack in the center of the oven and preheat oven to 375°F. Coat a 9 x 13-inch baking dish with nonstick cooking spray and set aside. Cook the beans in a microwave-safe dish according to package directions. Drain thoroughly.

2. In a large bowl, fold together the celery, mayonnaise, soup, pimentos, scallions, salt, paprika, lemon juice, and basil until well combined. Fold in the chicken, rice, beans, and peas. Spread the mixture in the prepared dish.

3. Unfold the puff pastry sheet on a lightly floured work surface. Roll the pastry out to measure about 15 x 12 inches. Fold the pastry in half lengthwise. Cut 1/4-inch slits down the length of the fold and cut a large X in the center of the fold. Carefully lay the pastry over the filling, pressing it against the sides to seal. Pinch the pastry along the sides to make an attractive edge. Brush with the melted butter.

4. Bake for about 45 minutes or until the pastry is golden brown and the filling is bubbly. Allow the pie to sit for 10 to 15 minutes, then serve.

1/2 pound (8 ounces) frozen cut green beans
1 cup sliced celery
3/4 to 1 cup mayonnaise
1 (10 3/4-ounce) can condensed cream of chicken soup
1 (2-ounce) jar chopped pimentos, well drained
3 scallions, trimmed, sliced
1/4 teaspoon salt
1/4 teaspoon paprika
1 tablespoon lemon juice
1 tablespoon dried basil or herbes de Provence
3 to 4 cups chopped cooked chicken
1 cup cooked rice
1 cup frozen peas, thawed
1 frozen puff pastry sheet (from a 17.3-ounce box), thawed
1 tablespoon butter, melted

Overnight Free-Form Onion and Mozzarella Pies

1 teaspoon dried thyme
1 tablespoon chopped fresh
  parsley leaves
1 tablespoon all-purpose
  flour
1 (1-ounce) envelope
  dehydrated onion soup
  mix
1 large egg, slightly beaten
1 cup half-and-half
2 cups shredded mozzarella
  (8 ounces)
1 medium sweet onion, such
  as Walla Walla or Vidalia,
  halved, thinly sliced
1 (15-ounce) package
  refrigerated pie crusts
1 large egg yolk, slightly
  beaten
Pinch of salt
1 tablespoon water

Onion and mozzarella pies make a great Sunday night supper. They can also be cut into small pieces and served as an appetizer. Sweet onions, such as Walla Walla, Vidalia, Bermuda, and OSO Sweet, have a smooth, almost sweet taste as contrasted with regular yellow onions.

1. Combine the thyme, parsley, flour, soup mix, egg, and half-and-half in a medium bowl. Stir in the mozzarella and onion. Cover and refrigerate overnight. (The mixture should thicken; if it is runny, strain off the excess liquid.)

2. Preheat oven to 375°F. Line two 15 1/2 x 10-inch baking sheets with aluminum foil and coat with nonstick cooking spray.

3. Unfold a pie crust on each pan. Form a rim on the pie crust by folding over 1-inch of dough along the edge.

4. Fill each pie crust with half of the onion mixture, spreading it evenly to the rim.

5. Whisk the egg yolk with the salt and water. Brush the pie crust rim with the egg wash.

6. Bake for 25 to 30 minutes or until the crusts of both pies are golden brown. Allow the pies to cool for 5 minutes before cutting into wedges and serving.

Meatball Pizza Casserole

By using frozen cooked meatballs, refrigerated pizza crust, a jar of tomato-basil sauce, and some dried herbs from your spice cabinet, you'll have this casserole ready for the table in no time.

1. Position the rack in the middle of the oven and preheat oven to 375°F. Coat a 9 x 13-inch baking dish with nonstick cooking spray.

2. Place the tomato and basil sauce, Italian seasoning, and meatballs in a saucepan. Partially cover, and heat until the meatballs are defrosted, the sauce is bubbly, and the cheese is golden brown in several places.

3. Remove the pizza crust from the can and press into the prepared baking dish. Push the dough up the sides. Prick all over with the tines of a fork. Spread 1 1/2 cups of the cheese on the crust. Ladle in half the meatballs with a little sauce. Sprinkle the remainder of the cheese over the meatballs.

4. Bake for 30 to 40 minutes, or until the crust is golden and cooked on the bottom and sides, and the cheese is bubbly and melted.

5. Transfer the dish to a cooling rack. Allow the casserole to sit about 15 minutes, then cut into squares. Serve with the remainder of the meatballs and sauce.

2 (26-ounce) jars tomato and basil sauce

2 tablespoons dried Italian seasoning

2 cups (about 32 to 35 meatballs or 1/2 bag) frozen cooked cocktail meatballs

1 (13.8-ounce) can refrigerated pizza crust

4 cups shredded mozzarella cheese (about 1 pound)

Red and White Clam Pizza

1 (13.8-ounce) can
  refrigerated pizza crust
2 tablespoons olive oil
2 large garlic cloves, minced
1 (14.5-ounce) can petite
  diced tomatoes, well
  drained
1/2 teaspoon dried basil
3 vacuum-sealed pouches
  (about 1 1/2 cups) whole
  or chopped clams, well
  drained, or 5 (6 1/2-ounce)
  cans chopped or minced
  clams, well drained
2 cups shredded mozzarella
  cheese (8 ounces)

This is a delicious riff on pizza using a sauce usually linked with linguine. Using refrigerated pizza crust topped with clams, canned chopped tomatoes, and plenty of mozzarella makes this a satisfying meal put together in a jiffy. Accompany this knife and fork pizza with a salad for perfection.

1. Position a rack in the lower third of the oven and preheat oven to 400°F. Coat a 12- or 14-inch pizza pan with nonstick cooking spray.

2. Unroll the dough onto the pan, pushing it to the edges and pinching closed any gaps. Prebake for 8 to 10 minutes to set the crust, or until no raw or wet spots are visible.

3. Warm the oil in a medium skillet over medium heat. Add the garlic and cook until it begins to color a pale gold, 2 to 3 minutes. Add the tomatoes, bring to a boil, sprinkle in the basil, and cook until thickened, about 4 minutes. Stir in the clams and cook 1 minute more. Pour the tomatoes and clams into a strainer to drain any excess liquid collected in the bottom of the pan.

4. Distribute half the cheese over the prebaked crust. Spread the clam and tomato sauce over the cheese. Sprinkle the remainder of the cheese on top. Bake for 20 to 25 minutes, or until the topping and crust are golden and the cheese is bubbly.

5. Allow the pizza to sit for 5 minutes before slicing into wedges. Serve piping hot.

Top Hat Sloppy Joes

This dressed-up version of the school-age favorite is served in a ramekin or crock and topped with a puff pastry square. Discount supermarkets stock 1-cup ramekins.

1. Warm the oil with the onion and garlic over medium-low heat in a large, deep skillet.

2. Cover and cook about 8 minutes, stirring a couple of times until the onion softens, but do not brown. Add the green pepper and cook 2 minutes, stirring. Add the meat and cook until it is no longer pink, breaking up large pieces with the side of a wooden spoon. Stir in the tomatoes, tomato sauce, ketchup, and beef broth.

3. Increase the heat to medium and bring the sauce to a boil. Reduce the heat to maintain a slow boil, partially cover, and cook about 30 minutes, stirring frequently. Add the Worcestershire sauce, vinegar, salt, and pepper; stir to blend. Remove from heat.

4. Preheat oven to 375° F. Place a 15 1/2 x 10-inch baking pan with sides in the oven.

5. Lightly oil the rim of the ramekins using olive oil. Ladle the filling into four 1-cup ramekins or crocks. Unfold the pastry sheet on a lightly floured work surface and cut it in half lengthwise and widthwise to form 4 squares of equal size. Place 1 pastry square over each of the 4 ramekins.

6. Place the ramekins on the baking pan and bake for 15 to 20 minutes or until the pastry is puffy, golden brown, and flaky.

7. Remove the ramekins from the oven. Using an oven mitt, place each ramekin on a plate and serve with soup spoons.

2 tablespoons olive oil
1 large yellow onion, chopped
3 large garlic cloves, finely minced
1 large green bell pepper, seeded, cored, chopped
2 pounds coarsely ground lean beef
1 (14.5-ounce) can stewed tomatoes, chopped
1 (8-ounce) can tomato sauce
6 tablespoons ketchup
1 (14-ounce) can beef broth
2 tablespoons Worcestershire sauce
2 teaspoons apple cider vinegar
1/2 teaspoon salt
1/4 teaspoon black pepper
1 sheet (from a 17.3–ounce box) frozen puff pastry, thawed

Shrimp Cakes with Hollandaise Sauce en Croûte

Shrimp Cakes:
- **1 pound cooked frozen small salad shrimp, thawed, rinsed, drained**
- **2 scallions, trimmed, thinly sliced**
- **2 teaspoons Worcestershire sauce**
- **4 tablespoons mayonnaise**
- **1 large egg, lightly beaten**
- **1/4 cup plain dry bread crumbs**
- **2 tablespoons unsalted butter**
- **2 tablespoons olive oil**

Coating:
- **3/4 cup plain dry bread crumbs**
- **2 teaspoons paprika**
- **1/2 teaspoon onion salt**

En croûte is a French cooking term meaning "wrapped in cooked dough." These delightful shrimp patties are sauced with Hollandaise and enclosed in a puff pastry crust. They make an elegant presentation for a special dinner. Avoid over processing the ingredients, the mixture should have some texture.

Hollandaise Sauce:
- **1 (0.9-ounce) envelope Hollandaise sauce mix**
- **1 cup milk**
- **1/4 cup (1/2 stick) unsalted butter**
- **2 teaspoons snipped fresh chives**

- **2 sheets (from a 17.3–ounce box) frozen puff pastry**

1. Combine the shrimp with the scallions, Worcestershire sauce, mayonnaise, egg, and bread crumbs in the food processor. Pulse on/off several times to chop the shrimp and mix the ingredients. Spread the coating mixture on a piece of wax paper.

2. Form 6 patties of 1/3 cup each from the shrimp mixture. Flatten the patties to about 1/2-inch thickness. Place the bread crumbs on a sheet of wax paper. Press the patties into the bread crumbs, turning them over so both sides are coated. Refrigerate the patties for 30 minutes.

3. Warm the oil with the butter in a large skillet over medium heat until the butter melts. Add the shrimp patties and cook without crowding, about 3 minutes. Turn the patties and cook another 3 minutes until they are golden brown. Place the shrimp patties on a plate and chill in the refrigerator.

4. Prepare the Hollandaise sauce according to the package directions using 1 cup milk and 1/4 cup (1/2 stick) unsalted butter. Remove the sauce from the heat, cool slightly, and stir in the chives.

5. Preheat oven to 400°F. Line a 15 1/2 x 10-inch baking pan with aluminum foil.

6. Unfold 1 pastry sheet on a lightly floured work surface and cut it in half lengthwise and widthwise to form 4 squares of equal size. Place 1 shrimp patty on each pastry square. Spoon a generous tablespoonful of sauce over the patty. Bring the corners of the pastry up over the patty and make a topknot by twisting the corners together. Place on the prepared pan. Cut the second pastry sheet in half and cut one of the halves in half again to form 2 squares; wrap and freeze the leftover puff pastry. Form pastry packages with the 2 squares and remaining 2 shrimp patties.

7. Bake for 15 minutes or until the pastry is puffy, golden brown, and flaky. Serve with additional heated Hollandaise sauce on the side.

Cakes and Breads

Warm breads and cakes evoke some of the best memories. Wholesome breads offer as much comfort as a warm fire on a cold day. Using packaged dough gives baking a fun, carefree feel, with simple treats popping out of their packages into pans as easy as 1-2-3. These recipes rise and bake into picture-pretty perfection all on their own, but they look as if a professional baker had spent the night in your kitchen. Whether you are baking them for brunch or as an afternoon treat, these delicious breads and cakes will be enjoyed by everyone in the family.

Orange-Butter Sweet Cake

Zest is the thin, brightly colored outer part of the rind of citrus fruits. Navel oranges yield the sweetest, most intensely flavored zest. Use a microplane grater (a metal strip perforated with sharp holes) to obtain the greatest amount of zest from oranges and tangerines. Avoid using the bitter white pith, the lining under the rind of citrus fruit.

3 tablespoons unsalted butter, melted

Grated zest of 1 navel orange

3 (8-count) cans refrigerated Orange Sweet Rolls with Cream Cheese Icing

1/3 cup soft golden raisins

1. Preheat oven to 400°F. Coat a 10-inch plain tube pan with nonstick cooking spray. Spread any foam using a pastry brush.

2. Combine melted butter with orange zest in a small bowl.

3. Arrange 1 layer of rolls, filling side up, in the bottom of the tube. Press half the raisins into the rolls. Brush with the orange butter. Continue arranging the remaining rolls, filling side up, in a staggered pattern over the first layer of rolls. Press the remaining raisins into the rolls. Brush each layer generously with the remaining orange butter.

4. Bake for 25 to 35 minutes, or until rolls spring back when pressed or a tester inserted in the center comes out clean. Turn the rolls out immediately onto a cooling rack and then again onto a serving dish so the cake is face up. Spread all the icing over the hot cake. Serve immediately, using 2 large forks to pull rolls apart.

Cinnamon-Raisin Honey Cake

3 tablespoons unsalted
  butter, melted
2 tablespoons honey
2 (8-count) cans refrigerated
  Cinnamon Rolls with
  Cream Cheese Icing
1 (8-count) can refrigerated
  Grands! Cinnamon Rolls
  with Cream Cheese Icing
1/3 cup soft raisins

This sweet breakfast cake is so fancy it looks like it came from a French or Belgian bakery, but it actually can be put together quickly right in your kitchen. If you can't find different size rolls in your supermarket, you can always use the same size.

1. Preheat oven to 400°F. Coat a 10-inch plain tube pan with nonstick cooking spray. Spread any foam using a pastry brush.

2. Melt the butter and honey together in a small bowl and mix.

3. Using the can of "big" cinnamon rolls, arrange them, filling side up, in the bottom of the tube, lightly pressing each roll to fill the bottom of the pan. Press a few raisins into each roll. Brush rolls with the honey butter. Arrange the remaining two cans of rolls in a staggered pattern, pressing raisins in the buns as you go along. Brush each layer generously with the honey butter.

4. Place pan in the oven and reduce the temperature to 375°F. Bake for 30 to 35 minutes, or until golden brown on top. If rolls brown too fast, tent loosely with foil and continue baking until the cake spring back when pressed or a tester inserted in the center comes out clean.

5. Turn rolls out immediately onto a cooling rack and then again onto a serving dish so the cake is face up. Spread with all of the icing. Serve hot, using 2 large forks to pull rolls apart.

Streusel-Topped Cake

Just the right size and delightfully fragrant, this cake makes a delicious surprise for weekend breakfasts, and it's so easily assembled using packaged mini-cakes. Make the streusel ahead and refrigerate it before unrolling and patting out the cake.

1. Position the oven rack in lower third of oven and preheat oven to 375°F. Place a piece of aluminum foil on a baking sheet and rub a light coating of butter all over foil; set aside.

2. Combine the baking mix, brown sugar, butter, and cinnamon in a small bowl and mix with a fork or the tips of your fingers until the streusel mixture is crumbly.

3. Unroll dough and place topping side up on the prepared baking sheet. Gently press the pieces together. Pat the streusel mixture evenly over the dough.

4. Bake for 10 to 12 minutes, or until the topping is golden brown.

5. Place the baking sheet on a wire rack and allow the cake to sit a few minutes. Slide the pastry off the baking sheet onto a serving dish.

6. Stir the icing with a fork and drizzle over the streusel. Serve hot, using 2 forks to pull apart into serving pieces.

1/2 cup boxed baking mix
1/4 cup tightly packed brown sugar
3 tablespoons unsalted butter, softened
2 teaspoons cinnamon
1 (13.9-ounce) can refrigerated Cinnamon Mini-Bites with icing

Fried Apple–Topped Cake

2 tablespoons unsalted
   butter
2 medium apples, peeled,
   cored, thinly sliced
1/4 cup tightly packed light
   brown sugar
1/2 to 1 teaspoon cinnamon
1 (13.9-ounce) can
   refrigerated Cinnamon
   Mini-Bites with icing

Fried apples seasoned with cinnamon and brown sugar tops this pastry. Most apple varieties are great for this recipe—Rome, Granny Smith, even Golden Delicious—but remember to adjust the sugar according to the variety used. Use the slicing side of a box grater to make thin apple slices.

1. Preheat oven to 375°F. Place a piece of aluminum foil on a baking sheet and rub a light coating of butter all over foil; set aside.

2. Melt butter in a medium skillet over moderate heat. Add apples, brown sugar, and cinnamon. Cook the apples, stirring, until they are soft, about 5 minutes. Gently chop softened apples in the skillet; set aside.

3. Unroll dough and place topping side up on the prepared sheet. Gently press the pieces together. Bake for 10 to 12 minutes, or until lightly golden and dough springs back when lightly pressed. Remove pastry from the oven. Spread the apple mixture evenly over pastry and return to the oven. Bake 5 more minutes.

4. Place the baking sheet on a wire rack and allow the pastry to sit a few minutes. Slide the pastry off the sheet onto a serving dish. Stir the icing with a fork and drizzle over the apple topping. Serve hot, using 2 forks to pull the cake apart into serving pieces.

Cold-Oven Breakfast Cake

This makes a nice surprise breakfast for early in the morning.
It's a sweet magic that's hard to beat.

1 (3-ounce) box instant butterscotch pudding
1 cup chopped pecans
1/2 cup tightly packed brown sugar
1 teaspoon cinnamon
2 (16-ounce) packages frozen roll dough, partially thawed, cut into 2-inch cubes
1/2 cup (1 stick) unsalted butter, melted

1. Coat a 13 x 9-inch baking pan or a 10-inch tube pan with nonstick cooking spray. Spread any foam using a pastry brush.

2. Combine the pudding mix, pecans, brown sugar, and cinnamon in a medium bowl. Spread half the dough cubes in the bottom of the pan. Drizzle 4 tablespoons of the butter over the dough and sprinkle with half of the pudding mixture. Repeat with the remaining dough cubes, butter, and pudding mixture.

3. Cover with plastic wrap and a towel. Allow the dough to rise in a cold oven overnight. The dough fills the pan completely when fully risen. Remove the pan from the oven when ready to bake.

4. Preheat oven to 350°F.

5. Bake for 25 to 30 minutes, or until golden brown on top. Remove the pan from the oven and invert onto a serving dish, allowing the syrup at the bottom to drizzle over the buns. Serve hot or warm, using 2 forks to pull apart into serving pieces.

Note: Instead of having the dough rise overnight, allow the dough to rise in a warm place for 60 to 90 minutes, or until doubled in volume, and then bake.

Dried Cherry Scones

2 cups boxed baking mix,
  plus more as needed
1/4 cup plus 2 tablespoons
  sugar
1/3 cup heavy cream
1 large egg, lightly beaten
Zest of 1 navel orange
3/4 cup dried sweet cherries,
  plumped in 1 cup hot
  water, juice, or tea
2 tablespoons unsalted
  butter, melted

Scones make a wonderful snack, as dessert served with fruit, or spread with jam and cream cheese for breakfast. These particular scones are especially delicious with the tart-sweet flavor of dried cherries scattered throughout the simple batter. Preparing a batch of scones means you can have them on hand in the freezer.

1. Position the oven rack in upper third of oven and preheat to 425°F. Line a baking sheet with aluminum foil and lightly coat with nonstick cooking spray. Spread any foam using a pastry brush and set aside.

2. Combine the baking mix, 1/4 cup sugar, cream, egg, and zest in a large bowl. Drain the cherries and lightly knead them into the dough, about 10 to 12 times. Turn the dough out on a surface lightly dusted with baking mix and shape into a 10-inch disc. Transfer the dough to the prepared baking sheet.

3. Cut the dough three-fourths of the way down into 8 pie-shaped wedges. Brush the top of the dough with butter and sprinkle with the remaining 2 tablespoons sugar.

4. Bake for 16 to 20 minutes, or until light golden brown and a tester inserted into several places comes out clean. Serve warm or at room temperature with soft unsalted butter and fruit preserves.

Pecan Sticky Buns

Always a favorite at any time of the day, these sticky buns are loaded with pecans and flavorful syrup. They bake especially light and tender, with a disarming sweetness.

1. Preheat oven to 375°F. Coat two 9-inch round cake pans with nonstick cooking spray. Spread any foam using a pastry brush and set aside.

2. Combine the brown sugar, corn syrup, cream, butter, and lemon juice in a saucepan over medium heat. Bring the mixture to a full boil and remove from the heat. Stir in the pecans. Divide the mixture between the cake pans, smoothing it evenly with a scraper.

3. Divide the rolls between the pans, placing 1 can of rolls in each pan over the nut-syrup mixture.

4. Bake for 15 minutes or until the rolls are golden and the nut-syrup mixture is bubbly. Remove the pans from the oven. Immediately invert each pan onto a serving plate, allowing the nut-syrup mixture on the bottom to drench the rolls. Serve warm, breaking the rolls apart with 2 forks.

1 cup tightly packed light brown sugar
3/4 cup dark corn syrup
1/2 cup heavy cream
2 tablespoons unsalted butter
1 tablespoon lemon juice
2 cups pecans, coarsely chopped
2 (8-count) cans refrigerated Cinnamon Sweet Rolls with Cream Cheese Icing (refrigerate icing for another use)

Spicy Puff Pastry Cheese Twists

1 (1.2-ounce) envelope
  savory herb with garlic
  soup mix
1/3 cup shredded Mexican
  cheese blend (about 1 1/2
  ounces)
2 teaspoons chili powder
1 (17 1/4-ounce) box frozen
  puff pastry sheets,
  thawed

Garlicky and well-seasoned, puff pastry twists make great nibbles at cocktail parties and also pair perfectly with soups and salads. You can make these through step 5, and then flash-freeze until needed for unexpected guests. For an elegant presentation, place the twists standing upright in a tall glass.

1. Preheat oven to 425°F. Line two 15 1/2 x 10-inch baking sheets with aluminum foil and set aside.

2. Combine the soup mix with the cheese and chili powder in a medium bowl. Remove 1 pastry sheet from the box and unfold on a lightly floured work surface. Sprinkle half of the seasoning mixture evenly over the pastry.

3. Remove the second pastry sheet from the box and place on top of the seasoned pastry sheet.

4. Roll the pastry sheets into a 14 x 10-inch rectangle. Sprinkle the remaining seasoning over the top pastry. Place a piece of plastic wrap over the seasoning, then roll the pastry to press the seasoning mixture into it. Remove the plastic wrap.

5. Using a ruler as a guide, cut the pastry with a sharp knife into 30 strips measuring 1/2 x 10 inches. Twist the strips 3 times, place on the prepared sheets, and place in preheated oven.

6. Reduce the oven temperature to 350°F and bake the strips until golden brown, 11 to 12 minutes. Serve hot or cold.

Three-Ingredient Beer Bread

This bread recipe is one of the easiest you'll ever find. It's perfect with soup and salads, and even makes great toast for sandwiches.

3 cups boxed baking mix
1/2 cup sugar
1 (12-ounce) beer, at room
  temperature

1. Position the rack in the center of the oven and preheat oven to 350°F. Lightly coat a 9 x 5 x 3-inch loaf pan with nonstick cooking spray. Spread any foam using a pastry brush.

2. Whisk together the baking mix and sugar. Pour in the beer, continuing to whisk. Scrape up from the bottom of the bowl and around the sides to make certain ingredients are blended.

3. Transfer the batter to the prepared pan. Bake for 60 minutes or until a tester inserted in several places comes out clean.

4. Allow the bread to sit for 5 minutes. Turn the bread out of the pan onto a cutting board. Serve hot from the oven. Slice the loaf with a serrated knife.

Poppy Seed-Onion Loaf

1/4 cup (1/2 stick) unsalted butter, melted
2 tablespoons dehydrated minced onion
1 tablespoon poppy seeds
2 (12-ounce) cans refrigerated Buttermilk biscuits

This attractive loaf comes together in minutes. For a flavor variation, sprinkle a little cheese or dried herbs on the top of the loaf before baking. For a sweet loaf, omit the onion and poppy seeds and sprinkle on cinnamon sugar, instead.

1. Position the rack in the center of the oven and preheat oven to 350°F.

2. Combine the butter, onion, and poppy seeds in a small bowl. Separate the biscuits and dip each one in the butter mixture, turning to coat.

3. Arrange the biscuits, standing on edge, in two rows in a 9 x 5-inch loaf pan. Brush the biscuits with the remaining butter mixture.

4. Bake for 25 to 30 minutes or until golden. Allow the loaf to sit for 10 minutes before removing from the pan and serving.

Mexican Cheese Bread

This tasty filling gives ordinary bread a great flavor boost. If desired, vary the types of cheese and the seasonings until you find several great combinations.

1. Preheat oven to 375°F. Line a cookie sheet with aluminum foil. Coat the foil with nonstick cooking spray and set aside.

2. Combine the cheese, mayonnaise, chiles, pimentos, cilantro, chili powder, and garlic powder in a medium bowl.

3. Dust a work surface with flour and lay out the bread dough. Roll the bread loaf into a 10 x 7-inch rectangle. Spread the cheese mixture over the bread, leaving a 1/2-inch border around the edges.

4. Beginning on the long side, roll the bread over the cheese mixture. Pinch the edges to seal. Place seam side down on the prepared pan. Brush with the olive oil.

5. Bake for 45 minutes or until golden brown. Allow the bread the cool about 15 minutes before slicing. Serve warm.

1 pound shredded Mexican cheese blend (about 4 cups)
3/4 cup mayonnaise
1 (4-ounce) can diced green chiles, drained
1 (2-ounce) jar diced or chopped pimentos, well drained
2 tablespoons chopped fresh cilantro or parsley leaves
1 teaspoon chili powder
1/4 teaspoon garlic powder
1 loaf (1 pound) frozen bread dough, thawed
2 tablespoons olive oil

Bar Cookies and Desserts

Layered bars bring a varied and creative touch to run-of-the-mill dessert trays, cookie exchanges, and countertop cookie jars. Easy to assemble and requiring little time, the following bar cookie recipes use two favorite refrigerated cookie doughs, while other doughs such as pie crust and phyllo dough make for easy and elegant desserts that make a lasting impression.

Store bar cookies at a cool room temperature for a couple of days in an air tight container or they can be frozen for longer stretches of time. Just wrap the cookies in aluminum foil and place them in an air-tight plastic storage bag for freezing.

Chocolate Chip Caramel-Filled Bars

Delicious, with a melt-in-your-mouth quality, these rich bars marry refrigerated chocolate chip dough and candy bars. Use either Hershey Carmello Candy Bar or Ghiradelli Milk Chocolate Carmel Candy Bar for best results.
The bars freeze nicely for up to 1 month.

2 (18-ounce) packages refrigerated dough for Big Deluxe Classic Chocolate Chip cookies

2 tablespoons all-purpose flour

10 (1.3-ounce) or 5 (4.5-ounce) caramel-filled milk chocolate bars

1. Position the rack in the lower third of oven and preheat oven to 350°F. Line a 9 x 13-inch baking pan with aluminum foil and coat the foil with nonstick cooking spray.

2. Spread 1 package of the dough to fit the pan. Use a smooth jar, glass, or your fingers to roll the dough evenly into the corners. Bake the dough for 15 minutes.

3. Break the second package of dough into pieces and place in the food processor. Add 2 tablespoons flour. Pulse on/off to mix the dough with the flour and make crumbles of different sizes.

4. Remove the pan from the oven. Place the candy bars side by side over the hot dough—in some instances, breaking the bars to fit the space. Sprinkle the crumbles evenly over the candy. Return the pan to the oven and bake for 20 minutes.

5. Allow the bars to cool completely, then lift up the foil and remove the bars from the pan. Cut into small squares.

Oatmeal Raisin Chocolate-Filled Bars

1 (18-ounce) package refrigerated dough for Big Deluxe Classic Oatmeal Raisin cookies
2 tablespoons all-purpose flour
2 (4-ounce) bittersweet chocolate bars

Chocolate and oatmeal, and chocolate and raisins are mouthwatering combinations. These easy cookies have a hint of cinnamon too, and are combined with bittersweet chocolate in a sophisticated bar cookie.

1. Position the rack in the lower third of the oven and preheat oven to 350°F. Line an 8-inch square baking pan with aluminum foil and coat the foil with nonstick cooking spray. Spread any foam using a pastry brush.

2. Remove 3 large cookie dough pieces from the package. Fit the remaining cookie dough into the pan. Use a smooth jar or glass to roll the dough evenly into the corners. Bake the dough for 10 to 13 minutes.

3. Combine the reserved cookie dough pieces with the flour in a food processor. Pulse on/off to combine and break the dough into crumbles.

4. Remove the cookie base from the oven. Place the chocolate bars side by side on the base, in some instances breaking the bars to fit the space. Sprinkle the dough crumbles over the candy bars. Return the pan to the oven and bake for 18 minutes.

5. Allow the bars to cool completely, then lift up the foil and remove the bars from the pan. Cut into small squares.

Pecan Pie Bars

Chockfull of pecans and enriched with sugar and butter, these cookie bars are reminiscent of the ever-popular Southern pecan pie, with the addition of chocolate chips and coconut as well. For those who fear making a pie crust from scratch, the sweetened biscuit-mix crust used here is a dream come true.

1. Place the oven rack in the lower half of the oven and preheat oven to 350°F. Line a 9 x 13-inch baking pan with aluminum foil, leaving a 2-inch overhang at the ends. Coat the foil with nonstick cooking spray. Spread any foam using a pastry brush.

2. Combine the baking mix with the brown sugar and butter, using a fork to blend well. Sprinkle in the hot water and mix to a soft dough.

3. Gather the dough into a ball. Press the ball into the prepared pan, smoothing out the dough evenly. Bake for 10 to 15 minutes or until golden brown. Remove from the oven and cool on a rack for 30 minutes.

4. Preheat oven to 350°F just before making the filling.

5. Distribute the pecans over the crust, followed by the chocolate chips and coconut. Pour the condensed milk over the ingredients, using a knife or tilting the pan to spread it evenly.

6. Bake for 30 to 35 minutes or until pale golden. Cool completely. Cover with plastic wrap and allow the bars to sit overnight. Cut into small 2-inch squares and serve.

Crust:

1 1/4 cups boxed baking mix
1/3 cup tightly packed light brown sugar
4 tablespoons (1/2 stick) unsalted butter, softened
2 to 3 tablespoons hot water

Bars:

1 3/4 cups roughly chopped pecans
1/4 cup finely chopped pecans
1 (6-ounce) package semisweet chocolate chips
1/2 cup sweetened shredded coconut
1 (14-ounce) can sweetened condensed milk (not evaporated)

Rustic Free-Form Fruit Pies

2 sheets (from a 17.3-ounce box) frozen puff pastry, thawed

4 tablespoons fine, dry plain breadcrumbs

3 cups fresh blueberries

2 cups sliced fresh peaches

2/3 cup sugar

1/4 cup all-purpose flour

2 tablespoons apricot preserves, melted

1/4 cup turbinado sugar or granulated sugar

This beautiful dessert uses flaky puff pastry for its crust and fresh fruit for the filling. It's a free-form creation, meaning it is not molded in a pie dish. Supermarkets stock turbinado sugar in their baking section; it's one of the raw sugar remnants left after cane sugar is processed, but you can substitute regular granulated sugar.

1. Preheat oven to 375°F. Line 2 baking sheets with aluminum foil and coat with nonstick cooking spray. Spread any foam using a pastry brush.

2. Roll out 1 pastry sheet to a 12 x 10-inch rectangle on a lightly floured surface and place it on the baking sheet. Cut the points off the edges to round them. Sprinkle 2 tablespoons of bread crumbs over the pastry, leaving a 2- to 3-inch border all around.

3. Combine the blueberries, peaches, sugar, and flour in a medium bowl. Mix gently. Arrange half of the mixture in the center of the pie crust. Brush half of the melted preserves over the fruit. Bring the edges of the dough toward the center, pleating and pressing the pastry over the fruit and leaving an opening in the center. Sprinkle the tart with 2 tablespoons of turbinado sugar.

4. Repeat the above steps with the remaining pastry and fruit on the second baking sheet.

5. Bake the pies for 10 minutes. Then reduce the oven temperature to 350°F and continue baking 20 to 35 minutes more, or until the crust is golden brown and the filling is bubbly. Cut each pie into 8 wedges and serve warm or at room temperature.

Lemon Cheesecake Tassies

Tassie is the Scottish word for "little cup," and these captivating treats are a sweet mouthful. This easy dessert comes together quickly and uses already baked mini-phyllo shells stocked by supermarkets in their frozen foods department.

1. Remove the clear plastic wrap from the inner box of phyllo shells; set the shells aside in the container.

2. Beat the cream cheese with the lemon zest in a medium bowl on low speed until well combined. Stream in the condensed milk and continue beating until smooth. Beat in the instant pudding, 1 tablespoon at a time, until the mixture is creamy and smooth. Allow the mixture to stand 5 minutes.

3. Place 1 teaspoon of filling in each phyllo shell. Sprinkle the filling with about 1/8 teaspoon of crumbs. Place a piece of plastic wrap loosely over the filled tassies and refrigerate until needed.

3 (15-count) boxes frozen pre-baked mini-phyllo shells
1 (8-ounce) package cream cheese, softened
Zest of 1 lemon
1 (14-ounce) can sweetened condensed milk (not evaporated)
4 tablespoons instant lemon pudding and pie filling
2 tablespoons graham cracker crumbs

Notes

Notes

Notes

Notes

Notes

Notes

Acknowledgements

To my amazing, dear, sweet, and loving grandchildren: Hugo Vincent, Samantha, James Stanley, Thomas, Chris, Maura, and Audrey. You know what fun it is to play with dough and you've shown me how exciting and delicious the joys of the table really are.

Hearty thanks to my family members who shared their recipes and provided thoughtful input on the many dishes in *51 Fun and Fast Packaged Dough Recipes*: Jim, JH, Maria and Charles, Anna and Jeff, Judy and Hugo, Natalie and Dan. My thanks to Amanda Ray, Kelli Cobb, Sandi Macnemara, Helen Smith, Barbara Dod Whittle, Ann Schrader, Kim Jordan, and Dalia Binnie for taking the time to send me some of your favorite recipes.

The historical information relating to Bisquick Baking Mix, Poppin' Fresh Dough, Brown 'n' Serve rolls, and the Pillsbury Dough Boy originated on the user-friendly General Mills and Pillsbury websites.

It was a great pleasure reading the enlightening, helpful essays about the Holmes family, Chelsea Milling Company, and Jiffy products on jiffy.com.

Immense appreciation goes to everyone at Collectors Press: Lindsay Brown, my editor; Kevin A. Welsch, my designer; Lisa Perry, who doesn't miss much. And especially to CEO Richard Perry: You convinced me I could cook faster and love it. Thanks all!